Mind & Quill

Ella Nightingale

BookLeaf Publishing

India | USA | UK

Presentation by *BookLeaf Publishing*

Web: www.bookleafpub.com

E-mail: info@bookleafpub.com

ISBN: 9789357214599

First edition 2022

Ghost

A tornado surfaces around her
Every morning that she wakes
The conflict is constant
But the people she will encounter that day
Will never know how much courage it took her
to "paint her face"

She stands tall, fearless
Walks with poise and grace
She's quirky and peculiar
Different from the rest
Battles with the fear of the unknown
Constantly pushing herself to achieve her best

No one understands her
If they managed to get inside
They would see a little girl
Who wants nothing more than to run and hide

What's so good about her
You see when she wears her mask
Although from time to time it may fall
You'll never see through the cracks

Her smile is always there

When there's sadness in her eyes
She still pushes you to your limits
She knows how hard you try
She knows that you can do this
Maybe more than most
As she battles with those demons
Failing to let them consume her ghost

Every day's a challenge
She's thankful to get to her bed
To dream of the adventures
She going to next pull out of her head.

Broken Soul

When you peel back the beauty that coats our
bones
Beneath the liver and your lungs beyond the
heart that glows
There's a place that's hollow
Where no one dares to go
With no fire or spark for you to even follow

Under every battle that's been won or lost
Behind each decision where the coin's been
tossed
We think that it's our hearts that we neglect
With our consciences that allow us to reflect

Underneath it all if we peel back the pieces
Right to our bones not leaving any creases
There's a misty figure that's scared to touch
That's been neglected and looked over as
nothing's ever enough

Bullet wounds so deep you'd think they grew
amour
It's more than madness
It doesn't hate
But a reflection of karma

It may reveal itself to one that is the same
By a reflection from eye to eye of the internal
pain
But don't be scared if you're lucky to find
One that can see what's buried deep inside

When your body gets smashed into a million bits
Laid to rest in its final pit
It will stand there strong
Silent and broken
The whispers of your soul
The forgotten words that were never spoken

Safe Place

My mind to me is a place I can confide
To discuss the matters I don't want to hide
It is easy there, things locked in your head
You can't hurt anyone by words unsaid

Figures around you, they go by people
Some kind and caring
Others malicious and evil
You can't trust a soul as you will soon find
Not everyone has integrity just a smile full of
lies

Keep your thoughts in your head
Try and sleep through the sound
For one day it will be quiet there
When you rest in the ground

Your journey will continue if you stay true to
yourself
Rise above the ashes
Forget about everyone else

Solitude

In the still of this house
I become silent
As I roam where I want
I am who I want to be

I am not alone
I bask in this silence
Self love I give to my soul
At peace
I am free.

Regret

How do you even show regret?
Am I too proud to swallow my pride?
To show to those who I have wronged
That I wish I had tried

How do you even show regret?
Do I mask my feelings to shield my ego?
Put on a front that does not falter
My internal words you will never know

How do you even show regret?
Is it too late as my eyes start to crack?
No matter how much I long
The hands never reverse back

Time

Time is very unpredictable,
In one split second everything could change,
From that one action,
Triggering the wrong emotion could alter the
universe,
All we have discovered, all that we have known
forever.

Time is very unpredictable,
If one person would know it is me.
Life prepares us for love, heartache, loss
Even to some extent the meaning to live
But the problem with this world no one prepares
you for the reality of life.

If only you knew, 'reality' without a sugar
coating,
If only you saw 'reality' the truth,
If only you could look through my eyes and see
life.

The good, the bad, the things that can not be felt
And depending on one emotion or perhaps
mixed,

The things that one has been sheltered from.
Now is the time to ask yourself, is 'fiction' really
a fraction of the imagination that entertains our
souls
Or is it the truth, the mysteries of the universe?
The world which we live in, which we fear?
Is 'fiction' just a term which we have created in
fear of the unknown,
The fear of things we don't quite understand.

Unspoken

Words unspoken are the over thought ones
That were not said in the heat of the moment but
a reflection of what the heart felt
They may never be muttered the pieces that have
broken
Pride will stand in the way of them being dealt

Out Loud

Though it may only be breath
Words articulated
Out loud
Live longer than mortality.

Whilst lay in death
Agreements stipulated
Made mad men proud
But would change for sexuality.

Like Macbeth
Patriarchy paves the way for those manipulated
Sheep bowed
Now they question your mentality.

You

So many people become characters, lyrics,
poems and art
I wonder if they even know?
The canvas that we call 'art'
A ghost of whom we knew
Giving soul
Rebirth
To something new

Her

I look toward the sky
With the wings of a dove
You soar high
My love.

Lonely night's sets in sin
Guilt I do not succumb
Fire still flickers within
Ferocious when I held that gun.

Dreams

It's the closest I ever get to heaven
Shh, don't make a sound
I leave the monsters in reality
As I levitate off the ground.

My eyes become kaleidoscopes
I trace every colour and line
I wish I could stay here forever
My imagination has no concept of time.

Healing

It may not be a road well travelled
But one you walk alone
When your heart has unravelled
Your mind gets lost in the unknown.

There's no toy maker to fix you up
You sew your wounds by hand
And keep topping up your magic cup
Until it overflows and then you stand.

Fill your lungs with the air they crave
Healing takes patience and time
Give yourself praise for being brave
There's no mountain that you can't climb

Beauty

Beauty is not a reflection
Beauty doesn't stare back at you
As you reach the bottom of your glass
Beauty is that passion that burns for adventure
That constantly pushes you as it craves more
Beauty is in those lyrics that entertain the soul
That has you beaming when you open that door
Beauty is untouchable
More than the naked eye can see
Beauty is felt
Beauty is heard
Beauty is friendship, forgiving, supporting and
giving
Laughing until you can't laugh anymore
Beauty is behind those eyes when you've let
down that wall
In a world full of politics and war
Be that BEAUTY

Kindness

Kindness is a kiss from your soul
That could start a fire in another
On days when life has taken it's toll
It is a hug that can only smother

Kindness is entirely free
Something everyone can access
If you find the key and open your heart
You may change one's sorrow into happiness.

Firefly

Dear firefly,
In the darkest times you flicker,
Helping those who are gasping to breathe find a
rhythm.

You abandon when natural light is consumed,
To go back for another.
In the dark.

Untouchable

I hate that you are untouchable
I reach for your hand yet hold my own
I feel your warmth as we have our first dance
I open my eyes and I'm dancing alone.

Memories

I crave for you to think about me
Every time your eyes get lost in love stories
Romance was our favourite genre
Our reality splurged on all pages
Always
Now it's my least

Remembrance

I wear my poppy on remembrance day,
To salute the soldiers that did not stray,
You stood there on the battlefield side by side,
Fought for your country with honour and pride,
The battle fields covered,
There's no going back,
The petals are red,
The middle is black,
As the hearts of the fallen stop beating,
The hearts of the living stop breathing,
Lest we forget,
I smile with pride,
As I remember the beautiful poppies,
Laid to rest,
Side by side.

Innocence

In the stillness of innocence
My heart was so pure
I danced in the rain with silhouettes

I didn't care who you were
How you got here, your thoughts
We just laughed until we ran out of breath

Lemon Tree

I love hearing stories
The ones that come with age
I sit there and listen
Again and again

Dreaming of the past and what it was like
A life full of adventure
Kindness
No strife

There was this old woman a few doors away
She would sit and talk to me when I went out to
play
'Those lemons, those lemons, those lemons' she
said
She pointed to a hole in the ground where they'd
shed

She told me this story about her grandfather's
tree
That had survived wars
Fed mouths
Reaping for thee

She promised the seed was so far below

That you'd think there was nothing
But one day
It would show

She said 'oh my child, you have my word'
I waited for years
There was no lemon burst

As I grew older I forgot about the tree
Until one day my little girl came running to me
'Mummy, Mummy, that story you tell, about the
old lady?'
I looked at her 'well?'
"It's like magic Mummy, I thought it was dead
but when I rose this morning, it was there, it was
there"

As I gazed at my child
I knew magic was a gift
And although she never lived to see those
yellow tips
She was right all along that "crazy ole bat"
Her lemon tree story lived on after that.

Seasons of Change

The ice melts away. Their brittle arms become stronger, stretching towards the sky, as they strive to consume the overwhelming bright light which will stand before them. The trees unwrap; their children race to blossom, to feel the warmth, the blanket of love, which they would soon devour.

The bright light blinds as I step outside to smell the sweet scent of spring. As it stares through the clouds, feeling its hot, stuffy breath, like lightening to a tree, it strikes. It breaks away from the clouds, to own the sky, what is rightfully hers. I look up as she showers me with all her glory.

Scorching light reflects off the mirror-glazed pond, only to give the flowers the final breath of resuscitation they have longed for. They slowly stand up to absorb the light, rising out of their dirty moist beds, their little petals begin to peek.

Sky as blue as the sea, blades of grass are so green and sharp, one touch could kill. As the light breeze lifts, it cools down those which are ready to melt. Garden music springs to life. Bees buzz as they withdrew the pollen from the flowers that dance and sway to their beat. Beautiful butterflies unfold, flapping their wings loudly like beats to a drum.

Over in the corner, sitting on the wall, little robin redbreast whistles that joyful spring time tune, which I long to hear. Ice cream which has melted drops on to the heated pavement, only to sizzle from the warmth of their flames.

Months pass. As the radiant sky darkens, the days become shorter and the nights become longer. Garden gates begin to swing frequently. The midnight air overcomes, as the wind's whispers warn of his homecoming. Feeling his harsh, icy breath blowing on sensitive skin, I know his arrival will come.

As I woke this bitter Sunday morning, wiping the sleep from my eyes, I rose out of bed to open my curtains; to my surprise, a thick layer of frost had devoured what once was a luscious emerald carpet of fine blades of grass. This view I could only see after caressing the window to eradicate the dismal, disheartening view that was staring back at me, which was running down the windowpane, to only harm me with its cold, unforgiving, spine shivering touch.

The morning wintry air gathered around like a tornado ready to surface. Snowdrops daringly descended from heaven, carefully hitting the pavement only to perish. Jack Frost now owns the ground and everything that is fixed to it.

He strikes. Icicles shoot out of his strong solid masculine hands, only to open and soar through the intense air, latching on to that which was once beautiful. The snow continuously pours. As it covers me, its soft, sophisticated silk touch somehow warms me, which makes me smile. As the white pure sky paints itself black, the striking stars awake to expose their solid gold charisma. The blustery weather is silenced. For one moment and one moment only, I see winter's true beauty, the beauty of which has occurred from nature and seasons, the beauty that will be lost.

I blow out my last breath. Watching it coil in the air, the warmth of the kiss rises to touch the winter's sky. As the coldness continues to linger around me, I know it will not be over soon.

I must now be dead to the world, like the trees
that are at rest, sleeping peacefully, all snuggled
up, dreaming until spring time comes next.

www.ingramcontent.com/pod-product-compliance
Lightning Source LLC
Chambersburg PA
CBHW070730160726
48003CB00006BA/2431